EXETER CATHEDRAL

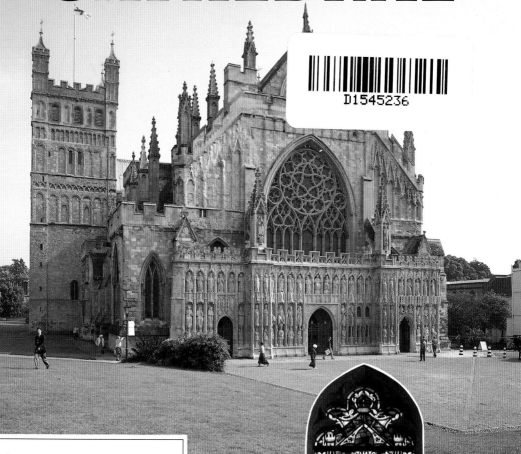

D1545236

Contents

Visitors' Guide	opposite
Dean's Welcome	2
History Chart	3
Roman and Saxon	4
A Building History	7
The Norman Cathedral	7
A Daring Vision	7
The 'New Work' Completed	10
The Finished Cathedral	13
The Reformation	16
Bells and Clock	21
Into the Modern World	23
The Blitz	25
The Cathedral Today	26

Above: ⑧
The north tower (with its near twin on the south), early 12th-century, is the earliest part of the present cathedral, and the Image Screen (late 14th- and 15th-century) the latest major feature.

Left: ⑪
King Edward the Confessor (1042–1066), England's royal saint, the founder of the See and cathedral of Exeter, personally installed Leofric in the Saxon minster in 1050. This light in the great east window is by Robert Lyen, 1391.

Dean's Welcome

Welcome to Exeter Cathedral!

You have come to one of the most purely beautiful of all English buildings. Quietly but firmly it holds its place as the heart of this ancient city. It leads but it does not dominate. The two great Norman towers are the visible sign that the cathedral has eight and a half centuries of life behind it.

But you have come to this house of God *now*. It is for you *now*. What does it hold for you *now?* It waits for you to discover its calm and tranquil atmosphere, fed by prayer and worship. The life of the cathedral rests upon prayer and the daily round of worship. If you come here seeking, you will find. You can add your own prayers to those which rise up to God from here.

As you come to this cathedral church and feel something of what it is, you are attaching yourself to its hundreds of years of history. You are making yourself part of its history; and it is making itself part of yours.

May God bless you in the pilgrimage of your life.

THE DEAN

History Chart

55–60	First Roman settlement.
4th century	First evidence of Christian worship.
1050	Bishopric under Leofric transferred from Crediton to Exeter.
*c.***1110**	Norman cathedral (with present towers) begun.
1270	Present cathedral begun.
1369	Completed under Bishop Grandisson.
1655	Destruction of the cloisters.
1665	Construction of Loosemore organ after the Restoration of King Charles II.
1688	William of Orange stays in the Deanery.
1840	Act of Parliament transfers cathedral assets to the parishes.
1870–90	Cathedral quire and nave restored by Sir George Gilbert Scott, and cloisters partially restored by J.L. Pearson.
1942	Exeter bombed. Cathedral damaged.

Roman And Saxon

Most of the cathedral which now stands was built between 1107 and 1350. But the site had been much used before that, as was revealed after the demolition in 1970 of the redundant 19th-century church of St Mary Major, whose east end was a mere 30 yards (27m) from the cathedral's west front. Archaeology uncovered the remains of a large Roman bath-house, a part of the Second Augustan Legion's fortress here about AD 60, in the time of the Emperor Nero and of St Peter, the cathedral's patron.

The first evidence of Christian worship on the site is a piece of pottery with the *Chi-Ro* sign, dating from the 4th century. St Boniface (*c.*680–754), the Saxon missionary in Germany, received education at a monastery here, so evidently from at least the 7th century there was a monastic or community church in the close. The foundations of this church, with surrounding graveyards, were revealed by excavation.

In 1050 Bishop Leofric, whose jurisdiction covered Devon and Cornwall with cathedrals at Crediton and St Germans, decided to make the Exeter minster of

St Mary and St Peter the cathedral of a united diocese which lasted until 1877. King Edward the Confessor came in person with his Queen to install him. The King and the Bishop founded a new community of twenty-four canons who were to follow a semi-monastic life, and whose successors have constituted the Cathedral Chapter ever since.

A foundation diploma, or formal description of the event, is preserved in the cathedral archives. At his death in 1072 Leofric bequeathed his library to the cathedral. This included the 10th-century Exeter Book of Anglo-Saxon poems and other writings. These two documents, like the cathedral community itself, are older than any building now visible.

Left:
This plaque on the Deanery wall records the extended knowledge of Roman Exeter revealed by archaeology in the close to the west of the cathedral from 1971–77.

Right:
An initial letter from the *Exeter Book,* the 10th-century collection of Anglo–Saxon writings and part of Leofric's bequest to the cathedral, in the cathedral library in the Bishop's Palace.

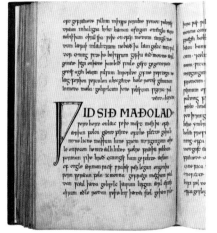

Left: ⑱
This sepulchral carving, the oldest in the cathedral, now in the Lady Chapel, is thought to be Leofric, the first bishop.

Right: ⑧
The north tower. The statue is of Exeter's Richard Hooker, priest and scholar, who defended the 'middle way' of Queen Elizabeth I's church settlement in his *Laws of Ecclesiastical Polity.*

The Norman Cathedral

In the time of the third Bishop of Exeter, William Warelwast (1107–37), a nephew of William the Conqueror, the Norman passion for building started a new Cathedral of St Peter on the present site. The old church retained the name of 'Great' St Mary, but these things were forgotten, and the Elizabethan John Hooker guessed that the Saxon minster was on the site of (or actually was) the present Lady Chapel. Versions of this error were repeated until the excavations of the 1970s.

The Norman work provides the base of the nave walls of the present building. The quire was shorter, probably ending in an apse. Still standing are the towers, the most remarkable feature of both the Norman and present cathedrals. Instead of a central or western tower, there are twin towers north and south of the east end of the nave. No other church has Norman towers in this position.

In the early 13th century the cathedral community acquired the form which has lasted in the main to the present day. The monastic elements in Leofric's intention did not materialise. In 1225 Bishop Brewer founded the office of dean, who presided over a secular chapter as an independent corporation. Under the south tower a chapter house was built for meetings and business – the only part of the cathedral in Early English style.

In the latter days of the Norman cathedral the quire must have been arranged much as at present. The upper stalls were for the canons, with the four principal officers, dean, precentor, chancellor, treasurer, at the corners. Each canon had his deputy or 'vicar', and there were 'apprentices' – choristers and others who might, or might not, proceed to holy orders. The main work of this body was to maintain the long and complex round of daily services. One piece of furniture has survived from those days – the carvings under the canons' stalls, called misericords.

A Daring Vision

In 1258 the new cathedral at Salisbury was consecrated. With its pointed arches and lancet windows it was, and remains, the great example of Early English. The new Bishop of Exeter, Walter Brones combe (1258–80) and his clergy must have felt the limitation and inconvenience of their own cathedral by comparison. A few years later they began a bold rebuilding which has produced the cathedral we know.

Important evidence about the work comes from an annual series of fabric accounts preserved in the cathedral library. Full accounts do not begin until 1299, but the work had begun before then. After 1334 the accounts are often either missing or less informative.

Work began about 1270, on the axis of the Norman cathedral but well to the east of it, with the present Lady Chapel and its flanking chapels of St John the Evangelist and St Gabriel.

Left and inset: (18)
The Lady Chapel, dedicated to the mother of Jesus, was begun about 1270, and originally had its own range of services. From 1657 it was the library; but in 1820 it was restored for worship, and is now used for daily services. It is a special place for silence and private prayer, with its modern statue and votive candles.

Below: (4)
The most dramatic of the cathedral's bosses depicts the murder of Archbishop Thomas Becket by four knights in Canterbury Cathedral on 29 December 1170. The boss was carved about 1340 and recoloured in 1975.

Bishop Bronescombe left directions to be buried on the south side of the Lady Chapel at what was then the limit of the new work, and his fine effigy, with a later base and canopy, is one of the cathedral's greatest treasures.

Under his successor Peter Quinil, or Quivil (1280–91) the Lady Chapel was completed as a first essay in the cathedral's distinctive Decorated style. The features of this are large windows with tracery varying from window to window but matching its partner opposite, and 'tierceron' vaulting, that is, stone ribs which start from the springers and link with the central rib, with carved and coloured bosses at the intersections.

Meanwhile the most characteristic feature of the cathedral was produced by the treatment of the towers. Their inner walls were removed to make them into shallow transepts, and their north and south walls pierced by large Decorated windows.

Above: ⑦
The screen (1317–1325), encloses the quire and supports the organ. The paintings are 17th-century.

Left: ⑭
The misericords, carvings under the quire stalls, are 13th-century, and the most famous is the elephant (now on display in the south quire aisle).

Left: ⑪
The Prophet Isaiah, in the great east window, by Walter the Glazier, 1304.

Right: ⑪
The great east window, the high altar with the Exeter Pillar and ambulatory behind.

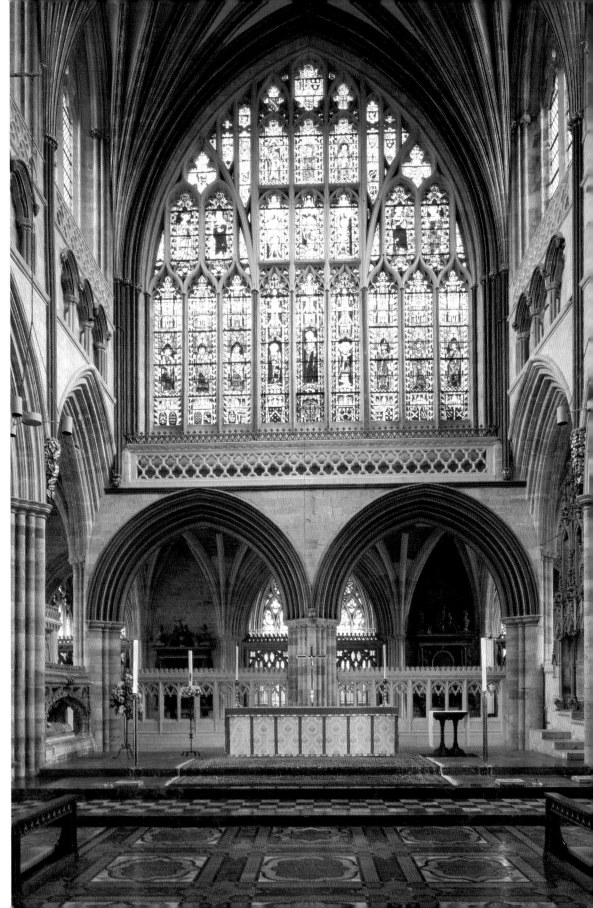

Left: ⑱
The sedilia, or seats for the clergy, on the south side of the Lady Chapel.

Right: ①
The nave (looking towards the great west window with its modern glass) is light, colourful and spacious.

Below: ⑤
The tierceron vaulting of the nave with stone ribs and coloured bosses. The Minstrels' Gallery is still used for music.

The 'New Work' Completed

In Bishop Bitton's time (1292–1307) the presbytery – the area of the high altar – was completed under Roger, master mason, and the style of the Lady Chapel received the two-fold adaptation which was to be used consistently throughout the quire and the nave. First, in the centre behind the high altar is the 'Exeter pillar'; sixteen shafts of Purbeck marble in a pattern which is thereafter continued unchanged. Second, the vaulting is expanded to three pairs of ribs on each side of each bay. From east to west it is the longest stone vault of its kind.

Walter Stapeldon (1308–26) was the cathedral's greatest episcopal benefactor, and after his cruel political murder by a London mob he was buried on the north side of the high altar he had given. Only the sedilia, or seats for the clergy, survive. Features of his time which remain are the richly carved stone pulpitum (the organ screen) and the canopy over the bishop's throne. This is the finest of its kind in existence. Both were executed under the direction of Thomas of Witney.

The 'new work' was completed in the time of Bishop John Grandisson (1327–69) who wrote to Pope John XXII praising the splendours of the cathedral's design.

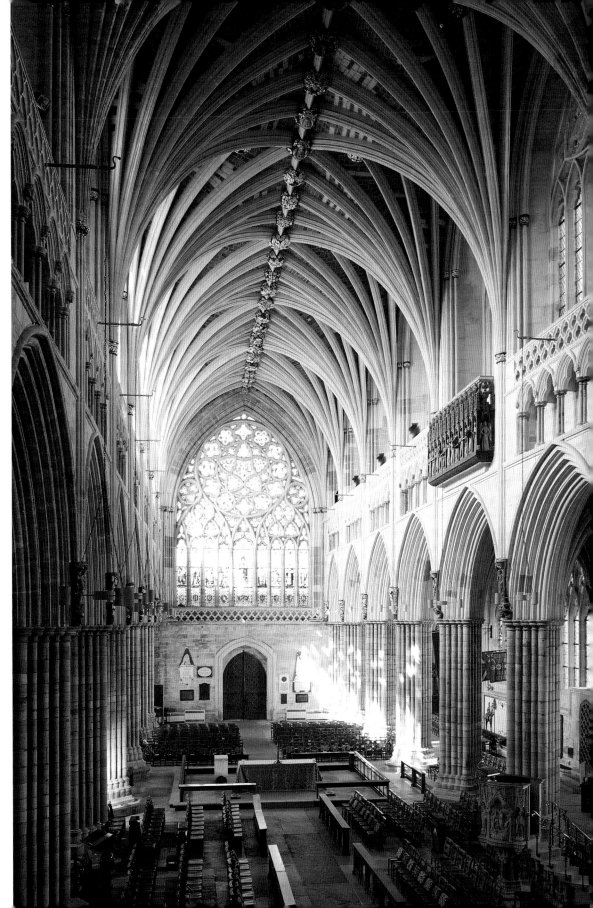

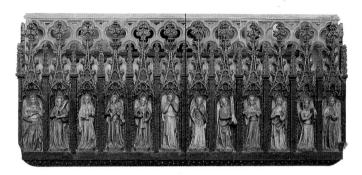

Records about the work on the nave are incomplete, but it seems that about 1350 the Minstrels' Gallery was constructed, with angels playing contemporary musical instruments. The last major feature was the Image Screen at the west front, evidently an afterthought and, to judge by the dress of some of the figures, modified a century later. The overall plan is not now identifiable, nor are many individual figures.

Grandisson was buried in a chapel built in the thickness of the screen south of the west door, but his tomb was a casualty of the Reformation.

The Finished Cathedral

Though the main work on the fabric was complete, probably by 1350, additions and developments continued. A complete four-sided cloister was built south of the nave, with a library above. The chapter house was reconstructed after a fire and its fine roof and upper part is mid-15th century. Its east window had stained glass which two centuries later was transferred to fill gaps in the great east window of the cathedral.

That window was reconstructed in 1390 because the stonework of a century earlier had decayed. The new window was Perpendicular in style – that is, the vertical mullions continue direct to the upper frame. Much of the glass produced by Walter and Glazier in 1303–4 was

re-used, but Robert Lyen made some new figures. Thus, with the glass later brought from the chapter house, the window has three distinct styles.

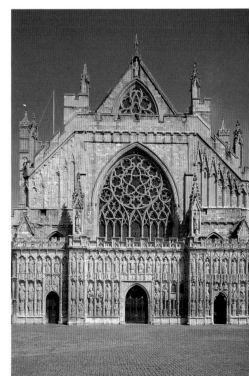

Right: ①
The great west window.
In 1904 a window was
inserted in memory of
Frederick Temple, Bishop
of Exeter 1896–85,
Archbishop of
Canterbury 1896–1902.
The glass was destroyed
in the Blitz and replaced
with the additional
commemoration of
Frederick's son, William,
born in the palace in
1881, Archbishop of
Canterbury 1942–44.

The south-east side of the cathedral, seen from the
garden of the Bishop's Palace.

The cathedral community generated two subsidiary groups with appropriate buildings. The Vicars Choral received a charter from Henry IV in 1401 and had residences and a hall on the north side of the deanery. Wealthy persons endowed chantry priests to say masses for the repose of their souls either at specified altars or in chantry chapels specially built. Precentor Sylke enclosed the altar of the Holy Cross under the north tower as his chantry about 1500, and the north wall was embellished with paintings of the entombment and resurrection of Jesus. The latter has survived to benefit from modern conservation.

Matching chantries were built at the east end of the quire aisles for Sir John Speke (d.1518) and Bishop Hugh Oldham (1505–19) founder of Manchester Grammar School. The chantry priests, or annuellars as they were known at Exeter, had communal buildings near St Martin's church.

The Reformation

The religious changes of the 16th and 17th centuries were not favourable to cathedrals. Monasteries were dissolved by Henry VIII and cathedrals, as clerical communities with an elaborate round of worship, were not so very different. All chantries were dissolved in 1547. The annuellars disappeared and their chapels were disused. But after 1553 Henry's daughters Mary I and Elizabeth 1, though differing on some matters, followed a conservative policy on the ecclesiastical corporations and the Dean and Chapter, with the subsidiary College of Vicars Choral, survived largely intact.

Nevertheless the cathedral was required to conform to national changes in worship. Stone altars were dismantled and side chapels neglected or used for other purposes. Images which had been revered were destroyed and wall paintings white-washed.

Below: ㉓
The tomb (much restored) of Hugh Courtenay, second Earl of Devon (died 1377), and his countess Margaret de Bohun. The Courtenays of Powderham, one of England's oldest noble families, have supplied two bishops of Exeter. The tomb, now in the south transept, was originally in a chantry chapel in the nave.

Right: ㉓
The tomb of Sir John Gilbert of Compton (died 1596), a half-brother of Sir Walter Raleigh, and his wife Elizabeth Chudley, in the south transept. It was recoloured in 1962.

Below: ⑧
The early 16th-century painting of the Resurrection in the Chapel of the Cross, north tower.

Right: (14)
The quire lectern, of uncertain date, was given by Dr John Bidgood, a local physician, in the late 17th century.

Below: (17)
The tombs of Sir John and Lady Doderidge in the Lady Chapel, are fine examples of early 17th-century work. Sir John, a noted judge, wears the official dress of his day, his wife the costume of a lady of fashion .

Exeter suffered less than many great churches. Its magnificent array of bosses and corbels is almost untouched. Only one statue seems to have been lost from the Image Screen. The stone carvings on the frieze of the quire screen were vandalized but replaced, probably in the 1630s, by paintings on stone. The reredos of the high altar, which had lost its statues, was treated in the same way.

The collapse of King Charles I's government in the 1640s and the consequent suppression of church authorities by the juntas which held power gave the cathedral its most traumatic interlude. The chapter was disbanded and the building handed over to the city council. They desired to use it for the worship of two favoured, but rival, groups. So an internal wall was built; the Presbyterians had the quire and the Congregationalists the nave. The cloisters were destroyed but some of the Exeter citizens prevented the dispersal of the library which in 1658 was housed in the Lady Chapel. When Charles II returned in 1660 the old constitution of the cathedral returned with him.

Left: (15)
The Chapel of St George, built as his chantry by Sir John Speke in 1517. With the Oldham chantry opposite, it is the last architectural feature before the Reformation. In the 17th and 18th centuries it was used as an entrance to the cathedral.

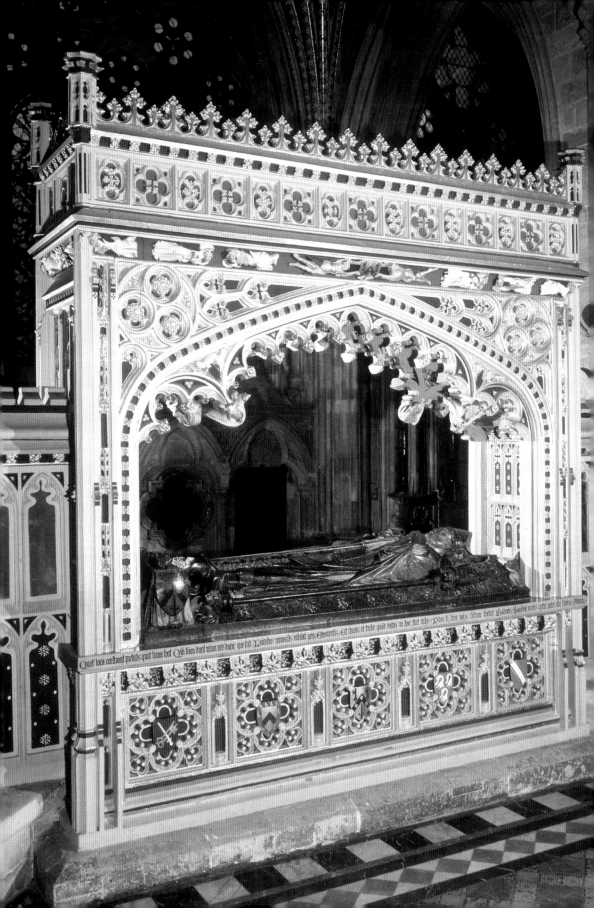

The Bells

There are fifteen bells in the cathedral. In the north tower the great clock bell, 'Peter', is the oldest bell of its weight in the British Isles. It weighs four tons, and was the gift of Bishop Peter Courtenay in 1484. It is now hung 'dead' and struck with a hammer, though it was swung when it was first placed in position. Today curfew is rung every evening on 'Peter', the number of strokes indicating the day of the month.

In the south tower there is the second heaviest peal of bells in the world, which has been described as 'surpassed by none in the kingdom either in weight of metal or richness in tone'. All the bells have names, many of which date from the 14th and 15th centuries; some commemorate the donors, others the founders.

One, known as the Doom bell, which has been in use for over four hundred years, may have taken its name from the fact that it was used as a knell when executions were performed.

The earliest complete list of existing bells, made in 1552, records that 'Peter' and four small bells were then hung in the north tower while eight bells were hung in the south tower. Though there are fourteen bells in the south tower, they are never used all at the same time, but give the possibility to ring on any number from 5 to 12 with choice of key.

The Clock

There was a clock in the cathedral as early as 1284, since it was then 'put in good order' by a bell-founder named Roger de Ropford; but no trace of this remains. The present clock on the north wall of the north tower dates from the last quarter of the 15th century and was traditionally the gift of Bishop Peter Courtenay (1478–87). At the centre of the large dial is a globe representing the earth. Round it revolves the moon, turning on its own axis to show its phases. The fleur-de-lys represents the sun, which, since this is a 15th-century clock, revolves round the earth in 24 hours. It points to the hour on the outer circle of figures and to the age of the moon on the inner circle, which is geared to revolve at a slightly slower rate.

The Latin inscription 'Pereunt et imputantur' – 'they (the hours) perish and are reckoned to our account' – is a quotation from Martial: Epigrammata, Book V, No 20. The upper dial of the clock was added in 1759 by William Howard, 'an ingenious mechanic of this city'. The works now on view, which have recently been put into working order, are a mixture of old and new. One 'train' almost certainly dates from the late 15th century; the rest from the late 16th and early 17th centuries.

Left: ⑦
The organ case was
made in 1665 by John
Loosemore; the rest of
the instrument has since
been subject to periodic
repair and rebuilding.

Below and right: ④
The font, of Sicilian
marble, has an oak cover
with eight inlaid figures
of Apostles.

Following the Restoration the cathedral acquired the organ case (1665) and font (1687). The year 1688 saw the dramatic arrival of the Prince of Orange, but the change of government did not alter the life of the cathedral. The 18th century produced increasing interest in the cathedral's architecture, now obviously 'antique' and increasingly in need of attention. In the early 19th century, under the architect John Kendall, there was much exterior restoration. Buildings abutting on the cathedral were removed to reveal its integrity and symmetry, and in 1820 the Lady Chapel was again used for worship, the library being removed to the chapter house. A new reredos was provided for the high altar.

Later in the century attention shifted to the interior which was given a thorough overhaul by the architect Sir George Gilbert Scott between 1870 and 1877.

Scott transformed the quire with a new set of stalls (incorporating the old misericords), a new floor of encaustic tiles and coloured marble, and a new reredos. He also pierced the outer bays of the organ screen and the side walls of the quire, allowing a view of the quire from the nave and aisles.

The rich altar reredos with its cross and carved figures was the subject of a legal dispute, but its vindication laid a ghost which had haunted the Church of England since the Reformation – the impropriety of carved figures. The eventual removal of the reredos to Heavitree in 1939 was due to taste and convenience, not principle.

The side chapels gradually came back into use, sometimes with original stone altars. A beginning was made on rebuilding the cloisters, but only one corner was completed. Meanwhile industrial smoke from the west quarter of the city turned the cathedral black and hastened the decay of the stonework.

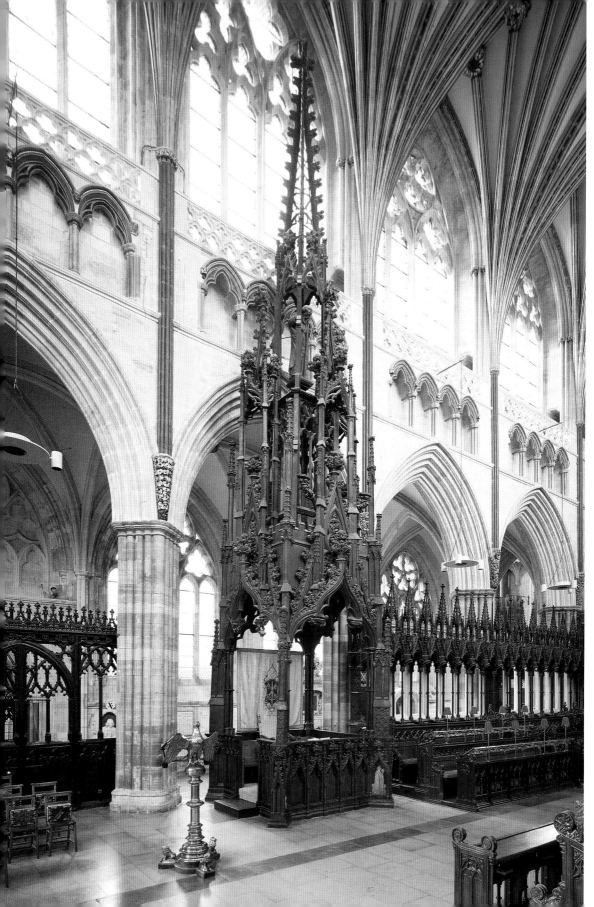

When war broke out in 1939 three of the cathedral's greatest treasures were removed to a place of safety. These were the glass of the east window, the effigy of Bishop Bronescombe and the throne canopy which was dismantled for the first time in its 600-year history.

The precaution was timely. On 4 May 1942 German bombers came up the Exe estuary and all but destroyed the ancient city of Exeter. The raid, on a place of historic interest, was unhappily of a type undertaken by both sides.

The cathedral had a direct hit. The double chapel of St James, used as a vestry, was destroyed, as were two bays of the south quire aisle. Most of the glass in position was shattered, and the wreckage throughout the quire was heart-breaking. Fears that the structure had been affected were happily unfounded, and work to repair the damage began as soon as conditions allowed.

Left: ⑭
The great oak canopy over the Bishop's Throne, dismantled and removed during the Second World War, was made in 1312 with wood from the bishop's estates.

Below left: ⑩
Sir Ninian Comper's window commemorating HMS *Exeter*, lost in the Java Sea, 1942.

Below right: ㉑
On 4 May 1942 a bomb destroyed the chapel of St James and St Thomas in the south quire aisle. The chapel was rebuilt and is now linked with the Devon and Dorset Regiment.

Herbert Read and his team salvaged thousands of fragments of wood and stone, and today only a practised eye can detect the signs of damage. The rebuilt chapel of St James has an inscription commemorating the destruction and rebuilding, and a window in the south nave aisle depicts the Exeter raid, with St Peter holding up the cathedral.

From the 1950s repairing war damage merged into increasingly intensive conservation of the cathedral's treasures. In the 1960s some monuments and sculptures were recoloured, but this treatment fell out of favour. From 1974 to 1982 the whole of the interior stone was washed, and surviving ancient colour treated and conserved. The Exeter Cathedral Preservation Trust from 1978 sponsored careful conservation of the Image Screen and the most extensive work on the south tower ever undertaken in its 850-year history.

The Cathedral Today

Right, above: ⑭
The Rondels, tapestry cushions that tell the story of the cathedral in its world setting. Completed in 1989, the Rondels have 14 million stitches.

Right, below: ③
The cloisters, now a refectory.

Right, bottom: ㉓
A stonemason at work.

Below: ⑦
An ordination in the nave. The Bishop of Exeter and the suffragan Bishops of Crediton and Plymouth face west as one of the Canons prepares to read the Gospel.

Far right:
The statues on the 14th-century north porch are the patron saints of the Allies in the First World War, given by Archdeacon Saunders in 1918 in thanksgiving for the survival of his two sons.

Large ancient buildings need continuous attention, which is the business of the Dean and Chapter and their surveyor to see that the cathedral receives it. Scaffolding may be annoying to eye and camera, but it is a sign of care, and today there are many authorities concerned to see that the care should be of the right kind.

The Dean and Chapter remain the cathedral's governing body, with the Bishop having certain reserved powers. Most of today's 'Greater Chapter' are parish priests working in the diocese. A small group, four or five including the Dean, work at and for the cathedral, with a large number of assistants, mainly lay people, some paid, some voluntary. The College of Vicars Choral ceased to be an independent corporation in 1933, but choirmen, boys and girls still sing the praises of God for which the cathedral was built, usually eight times a week (including three on Sundays). Said or sung, the daily services of the Church of England are maintained by the cathedral, which is often the host for special services, for the city, the county, the diocese, the judges, the armed forces, schools, colleges, and over a quarter of a million visitors a year for whom it provides stewards, guides, education centre, shop and refectory.

The cathedral is not financed by any outside body, civil or ecclesiastical. Its own property, once extensive, has been whittled away and much of it transferred to the parishes, so that maintenance is heavily dependent on voluntary contributions. Three independent charities exist to help meet the cost: The Preservation Trust (for the building), the Music Foundation (for the choir and music), and the Friends of the Cathedral, who can and do support most areas of its life.

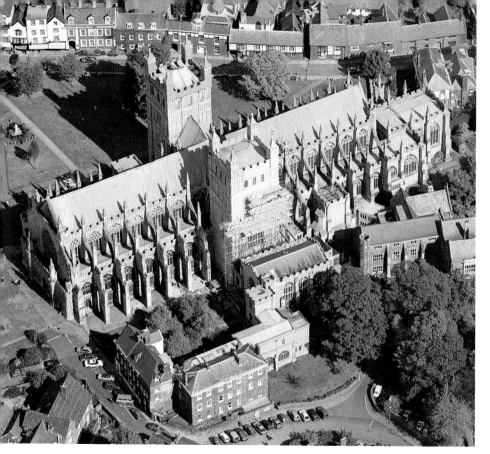

Left:
The aerial view gives an indication of the size of the cathedral building and the amount of maintenance necessary Its stone is mainly local, from Beer and Salcombe Regis, and in many places it has decayed. There has been considerable external cleaning to remove the industrial smoke of the last century but more needs to be done.

Right: ③
Christopher Webb's window in the south nave aisle shows Exeter in the Blitz, with St Peter holding up the cathedral.